My First Book about the Animal Alphabet of Asia

Amazing Animal Books
Children's Picture Books

By Molly Davidson

Mendon Cottage Books

JD-Biz Publishing

Read More Amazing Animal Books

Purchase at Amazon.com

Download Free Books!
http://MendonCottageBooks.com

 is for a Four Horned Antelope.

Mitternacht90 © <u>Wikimedia Commons</u>

They are the smallest antelope species in Asia; they can be found in Nepal and India.

Only the boys grow two sets of horns; one between the ears and one set on the forehead.

 **is for a Bharal (Blue Sheep).**

They live in the Himalayas in Nepal, Bhutan, India, Tibet, and Pakistan.

Bharal camouflage well with the rocky slopes of the mountains, and when they are seen, they freeze, to trick predators.

C is for a Bactrian Camel.

Bactrian camels live in the rocky deserts of Central and East Asia.

In the winter, when it is not very warm, the Bactrian camel can go weeks without water.

D is for a Dhole.

Yathin S Krishnappa © <u>Wikimedia Commons</u>

Dholes live in central and eastern Asia, Bhutan, Bangladesh, Cambodia, India, Indonesia, Laos, Malaysia, Myanmar, Thailand, and Vietnam.

Dholes can jump 7 feet straight in the air and are great swimmers.

 is for an Asian Elephant.

Asian elephants live in the tropical woodlands and rainforests of Asia.

Asian elephants are much smaller than African elephants.

Baby elephants are in their mothers for 22 months (almost 2 years) before they are born!

F is for a Red Tail Butterfly Fish.

It lives in the coral reefs around the Persian Gulf, Maldives, Japan, the Philippines, and Indonesia.

It swims about 9 - 50 feet down, and eats coral polyps.

G

is for a Gibbon.

They live in the rainforests of India, China, Vietnam, Laos, Sumatra, Burma, Indonesia, and Borneo.

Gibbons have one baby every 2 - 3 years, and it will live with its mother for up to 8 years.

 **is for a Striped Hyena.**

Striped hyenas live in the jungles of India, and western Asia.

A striped hyena's mane will stand up on its neck when it is frightened.

I is for an Indian Cobra.

Indian cobras live in Indian, as well as central and south Asia.

Cobras will bite; also they can shoot venom from their fangs, which gets in the eyes of their predators causing severe pain and damage.

 **is for Japanese Macaques.**

The Japanese macaques, also called the snow monkey, lives in the mountains of Japan.

In the winter, temperatures drop to 5°F, to keep warm they bath in volcanic hot springs.

 is for a Komodo Dragon.

They are only found on the islands of Lesser Sunda, Rinca, Gili Montang, Gili Dasami, and Flores.

They are the largest lizards in the World, weighing 200 pounds, with a length of 8 - 9 ft.

L is for Snow Leopards.

Snow leopards live in the Himalayan Mountains.

They are the strongest of all the big cats; they carry their kill high up into a tree, to protect it from other animals and to rest.

M is for **Malayan Tapir.**

Jeffery J. Nichols © <u>Wikimedia Commons</u>

They live in southern Thailand and Sumatra.

A Malayan Tapir's fur helps camouflage it, when it is lying down, it looks more like a rock.

 is for a Nightingale.

The nightingale spends the summer in the Asian forests, and will migrate to Africa in the winter.

The boys will sing at night to try and attract a girl. They also sing right before dawn to mark their territory.

 **is for an Orangutan.**

Orangutans live in Southeast Asia, on the islands of Borneo and Sumatra.

Their arms stretch out to 8 feet, that's longer than their body.

In Malay, orangutans means "person of the forest."

P is for the Peacock.

They are cousins to the North American pheasant, but they live mostly in India.

Only the boys have brightly colored feathers that they use to attract girls and to defend themselves.

 **is for a Qinling Panda.**

AilieHM © <u>Wikimedia Commons</u>

They live only in the Qinling Mountains of China.

Baby pandas are born weighing about 1/3 of a pound, having all white fur, and cannot crawl until they are 3 months old.

R is for an Indian Rhinoceros.

Indian rhinos only live on the Indo-Gangetic Plain, in India, Bangladesh, and Pakistan.

Both boys and girls grow one horn, made of keratin (what your finger nails are made of), when they are about 6 years old.

S is for a Siberian Tiger.

Siberian tigers live in the Sikhote-Alin mountain range, which runs through Russia, China, and North Korea.

In 1940, only 40 tigers lived in the wild, now there are about 540 Siberian tigers in the wild.

T is for a Tarsier.

mtoz © **Wikimedia Commons**

The tarsier lives on small islands in Southeast Asia.

One of their eyes weighs more than their whole brain!

 **is for a Uguisu.**

ISAKA Yoji (Cory) © <u>Wikimedia Commons</u>

This bird lives in mountain forests of Japan, China, and Korea.

They do not migrate, but are quiet and hidden in the winter, but they start singing when spring arrives, in Japan they are a sign of spring.

is for a Veiled Chameleon.

They live in the deserts of Yemen and Saudi Arabia.

Veiled chameleons change colors with the temperature, light or its attitude.

Mothers bury white, oval, hard eggs in the warm sand, until they hatch.

 **is for a Wild Asian Water Buffalo.**

Wild Asian water buffalo live in India, Nepal, Bhutan, Thailand, and Cambodia.

Boys and girls both have horns, which can spread to over 6 feet apart.

 **is for a Xiaosaurus.**

The Xiaosaurus, was a dinosaur that lived over 163 million years ago; its fossils have been found in China.

They was a small lizard like, plant eating dinosaur.

 **is for a Yak.**

Yaks live in the mountains of central Asia.

The yak is used by many farmers for pulling heavy equipment and for taking large loads over mountain passes.

Z is for a Zebu.

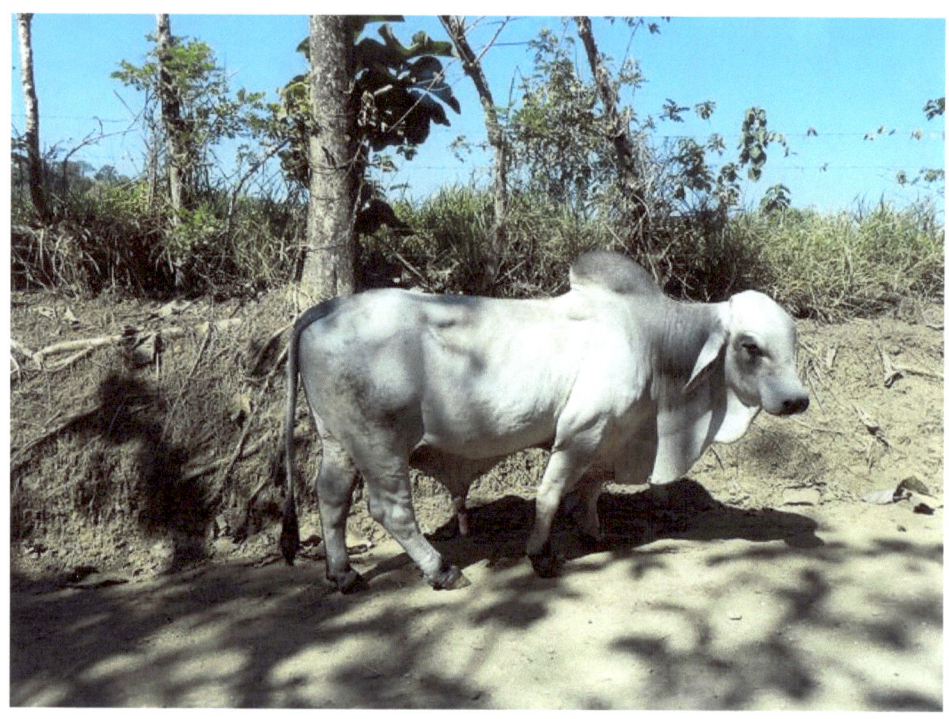

Zebu cattle live in the jungles of south Asia.

Zebus are about half the size of a regular cow, they only weigh about 440 pounds.

They have a large hump on their backs, and floppy skin on their neck, called dewlap.

Download Free Books!

http://MendonCottageBooks.com

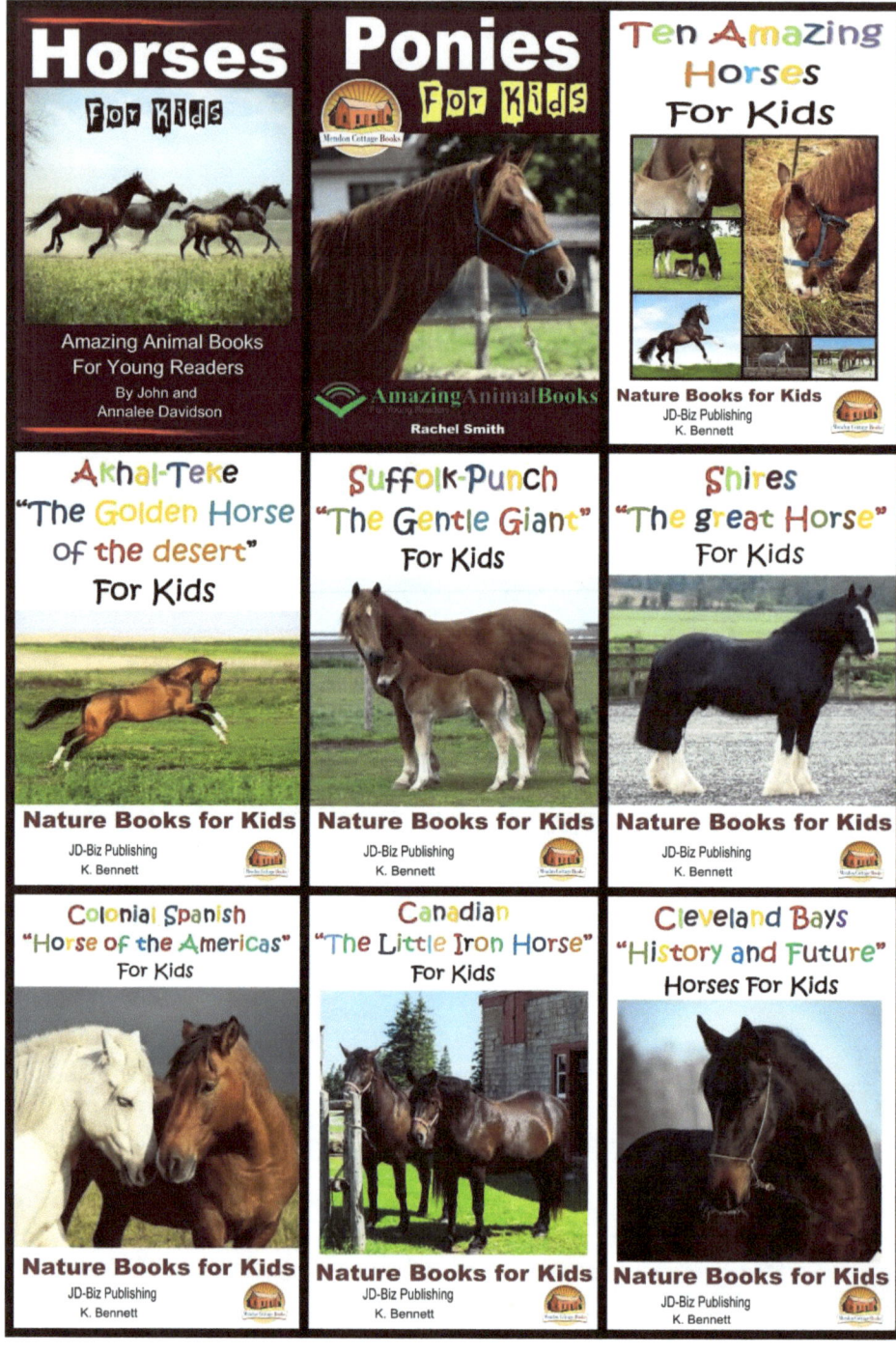

Our books are available at

1. Amazon.com

2. Barnes and Noble

3. Itunes

4. Kobo

5. Smashwords

6. Google Play Books

Download Free Books!
http://MendonCottageBooks.com

Publisher

JD-Biz Corp

P O Box 374

Mendon, Utah 84325

http://www.jd-biz.com/

www.ingramcontent.com/pod-product-compliance
Lightning Source LLC
Chambersburg PA
CBHW050908290526
45792CB00002B/738